Project-Based Learning Tasks

for Common Core State Standards, Grades 6–8

Authors: Schyrlet Cameron and Carolyn Craig

Editors: Mary Dieterich and Sarah M. Anderson

Proofreader: Margaret Brown

COPYRIGHT © 2014 Mark Twain Media, Inc.

ISBN 978-1-62223-463-9

Printing No. CD-404214

Mark Twain Media, Inc., Publishers
Distributed by Carson-Dellosa Publishing LLC

Visit us at www.carsondellosa.com

Table of Contents

To the Teacher

Motivating students is one of the basic challenges facing middle-school teachers. Research indicates students are motivated to learn if the topic is interesting and relevant. *Project-Based Learning Tasks* is a dynamic approach to learning in which students explore meaningful real-world problems relevant to their lives. The project tasks engage students in learning that goes beyond recall and copying information. The tasks give students a reason for learning important concepts and skills.

The English Language Arts Common Core State Standards stress the importance of students being able to "read analytically, write effectively, speak and listen purposefully, and conduct research" and to "use technology and digital media strategically and capably." This book is designed to allow students to develop and practice these essential skills while creating high-quality; authentic products and presentations. Project tasks vary in length, from several days to several weeks or even a semester. Tasks involve students working independently, in collaborative teams, or as a whole class, researching an essential question, creating a multimedia product, and presenting the project to an audience.

The book contains six student-centered interdisciplinary units. The content of each unit is correlated to the English Language Arts Common Core State Standards. For each unit, the book includes the following sections:

- *Teacher Information:* identifies the project overview, objectives, integration of other academic skills, materials and resources needed, technology requirements, steps for managing the project, and Common Core State Standard correlation.

- *Student Project Planner:* presents project overview and directions for the students.

- *Mini Lessons:* reviews concepts and skills needed as a result of the project assignment.

- *Project Rubric:* explains the set of criteria used for assessing the project.

- *Student Self-Evaluation and Reflection:* asks students to think about what and how they are learning.

Common Core State Standards © Copyright 2010. National Governors Association Center for Best Practices and Council of Chief State School Officers. All rights reserved. For more information on the Common Core State Standards, visit <www.corestandards.org>.

What Are Project-Based Learning Tasks?

Project-based learning tasks are authentic learning activities. The tasks are content based and designed to reflect the types of work people do in the everyday world outside the classroom. The high-interest topics, such as security cameras in the classroom and legal consequences for plagiarism, lead students to develop valuable workplace skills, including communication and collaboration, organization and time management, questioning and problem solving, investigation and research, and self-assessment and reflection.

Using Project-Based Learning Tasks

Tasks address relevant issues and focus on research, writing, and speaking skills. They require students to use technology and digital media to create and present their projects to audiences beyond the classroom.

The project tasks can be effective at all grade levels and with all subject areas and instructional programs, including after-school and alternative programs. The projects are generally done by teams of students working together to solve a problem and formulate a solution. Projects vary in length, from several days to several weeks or even a semester.

How to Assess Learning

Student reflection and self-evaluation, along with teacher evaluation, are important components of each project. Student performance is assessed on an individual basis and takes into account the quality of the product produced, the depth of content understanding demonstrated, and the contributions made to the project.

Implementing Project-Based Learning Tasks

Step 1— *Introduction:* The teacher launches the project with an event such as a video, discussion, guest speaker, field trip, or scenario.

Step 2— *Essential Question:* The teacher presents a question that will be the focus of the project.

Step 3— *Research and Write:* Students research the essential question, discover answers, draw conclusions, and generate solutions.

Step 4— *Product Creation:* Students create a multimedia product to present their project information, such as a media kit, public service announcement, blog, web page, or poster.

Step 5— *Presentation:* Students present their project to the appropriate audience such as middle-school staff, parents, or community.

Step 6— *Evaluation and Reflection:* The teacher and students both assess learning and performance using a rubric, teacher feedback, and student self-evaluation and reflection.

What Is a Multimedia Presentation?

A multimedia presentation includes the use of more than one medium to present information. This type of presentation allows you to communicate your research information effectively with your audience through the integration of text, graphics, animation, sound, and/or video.

Common Multimedia Presentations

Advertisement	Diorama	Podcast
Album Cover	Documentary	Photo Essay
Award	Drama	Poem-Rap
Banner	Editorial	Portfolio
Blog	Email	Postcard
Blog Radio	Exhibit	Poster
Blueprint	Graphic Novel	Radio Broadcast
Board Game	Guide Book	Reenactment
Book Club	Demonstration	Science Fair Project
Book Trailer	Interviews	Scrapbook
Brochure	Invention	Simulation
Exhibit	Journal	Slide Show
Bulletin Board	Letter	Song
Cartoon	Magazine	Soundtrack
Charts or Graphs	Model	Speech
Cheer	Movie Trailer	Venn Diagram
Classified Ad	Mural	Video
Collection	Museum Display	Video Conference
Comic Book	Musical Performance	Virtual Tour
Comic Strip	Newscast	Webinar
Commercial	Newspaper Article	Website
Debate	Panel Discussion	Yearbook

Multimedia Presentation Tools

There are many online tools for creating and sharing multimedia presentations.

Check Out These Sites

Animoto: turns still photos, music, and videos into video presentations

Audioboo: a site that allows students to create a simple image and five-minute audio presentation

BibMe: a site that offers an easy-to-use automatic bibliography maker

Capzles: a site for creating time lines with customized backgrounds

Edublogs: a site that allows students to easily create and manage blogs, quickly customize designs, and include videos, photos, and podcasts

Glogster: a site that allows students to create with text, images, graphics, music, video, and more

Jing: an online program that allows students to create annotated screenshots and narrated screencasts up to five minutes long

Kerpoof: a site for creating fully animated comics

Museumbox: a site that provides the tools students need to build an argument or description of an event, person, or historical period by placing items in a virtual box

NCES Kids' Zone: a site for creating graphs and charts

Prezi: a site that allows students to work individually or collaboratively creating text, images, and videos

SchoolTube: An online site for schools to upload, watch, and share videos

VoiceThread: a site that allows the user to combine pictures, videos, and audio to create a multimedia project (This is a subscription site, so you may want to use alternate free sites.)

Wiki: a classroom website where students can collaborate on a group report and/or share the results of their research and projects

Zoho Notebook: a site that allows students to create multi-page presentations; this site also contains a built-in audio and video recorder

Teacher Page

Unit: Student Handbook

Project Overview

Students will create a new design for one section of the student handbook. Students will incorporate informational text features into their design. Students will use word processing and graphic programs to design the section.

Project Objectives

When students complete this project, they will be able to use text features effectively, conduct a survey and interpret the results, and use technology to redesign a section of the student handbook. Students will collaborate with peers to create and share a multimedia presentation.

Integration of Academic Skills

- Math—conduct and graph survey results
- Language Arts—read information in student handbook
- Technology—use computer word-processing and graphic programs
- Science—interpret data and draw conclusions

Primary Common Core State Standards (CCSS) Addressed:

ELA-Literacy.RI.6.5 Analyze how a particular sentence, paragraph, chapter, or section fits into the overall structure of a text and contributes to the development of the ideas.

ELA-Literacy.W.6.6 Use technology, including the Internet, to produce and publish writing as well as to interact and collaborate with others; demonstrate sufficient command of keyboarding skills to type a minimum of three pages in a single sitting.

ELA-Literacy.RI.7.5: Analyze the structure an author uses to organize a text including how the major sections contribute to the whole and to the development of the ideas.

ELA-Literacy.W.7.6 Use technology, including the Internet, to produce and publish writing and link to and cite sources as well as to interact and collaborate with others, including linking to and citing sources.

ELA-Literacy.RI.8.5: Analyze in detail the structure of a specific paragraph in a text, including the role of particular sentences in developing and refining a key concept.

ELA-Literacy.W.8.6 Use technology, including the Internet, to produce and publish writing and present the relationships between information and ideas efficiently as well as to interact and collaborate with others.

© Copyright 2010. National Governors Association Center for Best Practices and Council of Chief State School Officers. All rights reserved.

Introductory Event

1. *Scenario:* The faculty is concerned that students are not reading the student handbook. They want to know what can be done to motivate students to read the content.
2. *Activity:* The teacher displays a variety of magazines. Each student selects a magazine and is given a few minutes to examine the contents. As a whole class, students identify the different features used by editors to make a magazine attractive to readers.
3. *Activity:* Students examine the student handbook. As a whole class, students compare the features used in the handbook with the magazines.

Essential Question

What can be done to the student handbook to encourage students to read the content?

Project Task

Redesign a section of the school's student handbook to make it more appealing to readers.

Product

Multimedia presentation of survey results and redesigned section of the student handbook.

Materials/Resources Needed

1. Variety of magazines, textbooks, newspaper editorials, biographies, and game instructions
2. Student handbooks
3. "Student Project Planner" (handout)
4. "What Is a Multimedia Presentation?" and "Multimedia Presentation Tools" (handouts)
5. "Identifying Organizational Text Structures" (mini lesson handout)
6. "Text Features Scavenger Hunt" (mini lesson handout)
7. "The Ins and Outs of Graphing" (mini lesson handout)
8. "Survey Planner" (activity handout)
9. "Project Rubric" and "Project Self-Evaluation and Reflection" (assessment handout)

Technology

Computer with word-processing, presentation, and graphic programs; Internet connections; and printers.

Internet Tools for Creating a Multimedia Presentation

Animoto <http://animoto.com/education/classroom> This site turns still photos, music, and videos into video presentations.
Prezi <http://prezi.com> This site allows student to go 'outside the box' to create presentations.
NCES Kids' Zone <http://nces.ed.gov/nceskids/createagraph> This site allows students to create graphs and charts.

Managing the Project

Step 1:   Activity—Launch introductory event, discuss the essential question, present project task and required product.
Step 2:   Review—"Project Rubric" and "Project Self-Evaluation and Reflection" handouts.
Step 3:   Review—"Student Project Planner" handout.
Step 4:   Activity—Students form teams. They review the school's student handbook.
Step 5:   Mini lessons—"Identifying Organizational Text Structures," "Text Features Scavenger Hunt," "ABCs of Conducting a Survey," and "The Ins and Outs of Graphing" handouts.
Step 6:   Activity—Student teams plan and conduct a survey. Students complete the "Survey Planner" handouts.
Step 7:   Mini lesson—"What Is a Multimedia Presentation?" (page 3) and "Multimedia Presentation Tools" (page 4) handouts.
Step 8:   Activity—Student teams redesign a section of the student handbook using appropriate text features. They use computer word-processing and graphic programs to design a section.
Step 9:   Activity—Student teams create a multimedia presentation of the survey results and redesigned section of handbook.
Step 10: Activity—Student teams give presentations to school principal and handbook committee.

Project Evaluation

1. The teacher completes the "Project Rubric" for each team.
2. Each student completes the "Project Self-Evaluation and Reflection" handout.
3. Teacher/student conferences are held to discuss the completed evaluations.

Student Project Planner

Question: How can the student handbook be redesigned to encourage students to read the content?

Project: Create a new design for one section of the student handbook. Incorporate informational text features into the design. Use word processing and graphic programs to design the section.

Steps

Step 1: Review the "Project Rubric" and "Project Self-Evaluation and Reflection" handouts.

Step 2: Review characteristics of informational text. Complete the "Identifying Organizational Text Structures" and "Text Feature Scavenger Hunt" handouts.

Step 3: Conduct a survey of the student body to determine why students are not reading the school's student handbook. Read the "ABCs of Conducting a Survey" handout and complete the "Survey Planner" handout.

Step 4: Select a section of the student handbook to redesign. Use the survey results to plan the text features you will include. Use computer word-processing and graphic programs to design the section.

Step 5: Review the "What Is a Multimedia Presentation?" and "Multimedia Presentation Tools" handout.

Step 6: Create and present a multimedia presentation of survey results and redesigned section of handbook to the school principal and handbook committee.

Step 7: Complete the "Project Self-Evaluation and Reflection" handout.

Name: _____   Date: _____

Project Rubric

Project Components	Below Proficiency 1	Nearing Proficient 2	Proficient 3	Advanced 4
Conducting Survey and Graphing Results	Incomplete.	Inappropriate population, questions have little connection to topic, and/or inappropriate type of graph.	Few errors in writing and conducting survey and/or construction and labeling of graph.	Appropriate population, questions are relevant and clearly stated. The appropriate graph is used for the data and the audience. The graph is easy to read and understand.
Organization of Content	Content lacks logical sequence of information. The layout is cluttered and confusing.	Content lacks logical sequence of information or the layout is cluttered and confusing.	Content is written with logical sequence. Layout is organized.	Information is presented in a way that is highly interesting to audience. Layout is organized with appropriate headings.
Mechanics	Many errors in spelling, capitalization, punctuation, and/or grammar.	Careless or distracting errors in spelling, capitalization, punctuation, and/or grammar.	Text is written with little need for editing in spelling, capitalization, punctuation, and/or grammar.	Text has no errors in spelling, capitalization, punctuation, or grammar.
Text Features	Features do not support content.	Features weakly support content.	Features support content.	Features support and reinforce content.
Presentation	Presentation was disjointed and interest level was low.	Majority of presentation was disjointed and interest level was low.	Majority of the presentation flowed and was interesting.	Presentation flowed well, kept the attention of the audience, and was very interesting.

Teacher Comments: _____

_____

Name: _____ Date: _____

Project Self-Evaluation and Reflection

1. Write a brief summary of the project. _____
    _____
    _____
    _____
    _____

2. What challenges did you face in completing this project? Explain, giving examples and
    details to support your answer. _____
    _____
    _____
    _____

3. List some of the things you learned while working on the project.
    _____
    _____
    _____

4. What did you like best about your final project? Cite examples and details to support your
    answer. _____
    _____
    _____
    _____

5. What did you like least about the final project? Cite examples and details to support your
    answer. _____
    _____
    _____
    _____

6. I would rate my work on the project (Excellent / Good / Fair / Poor). Explain, using
    examples and details to support your answer.
    _____
    _____
    _____

Name: _____

Date: _____

Identifying Organizational Text Structures

Text structures are organizational patterns used to break information down into parts that can be easily understood by the reader. Knowing the way the text is organized can help you focus your attention on key concepts and better understand what you are reading.

Directions: Collect a magazine article, newspaper editorial, biography, textbook, and game instructions. Study the Common Organizational Text Structures chart to determine how the text was organized in each source. Use the information to complete the graphic organizer below.

Common Organizational Text Structures

Comparison/Contrast	Classification	Chronological/Sequential	Argument/Support
examines how concepts and events are alike and different	divides topics into related categories or groups	arranges information into chronological order or is a list of steps in a process	states a point of view and supports it with details or evidence
Definition	**Cause/Effect**	**Problem/Solution**	**Description**
introduces and explains a word or concept	presents a major idea or event and resulting effects	states a problem and gives possible solutions	describes something using details and/or examples

Text Structure Graphic Organizer

Type of Text	Evidence of Structure?			
Magazine article				
Textbook				
Newspaper editorial				
Biography				
Game Instructions				

Name: _____ Date: _____

Text Feature Scavenger Hunt

Text features are used to help the reader locate and understand information. They are often found in magazines, newspapers, textbooks, web pages, and other forms of informational text.

Directions: Select a magazine and complete the chart.

The
RIGHT BITE

Table of Contents

F E A T U R E S

7   Apple Season
     Bake or Bite?

14 Interview:
     Chef Claude

23 Herb Chart
     Cut & Keep

From Our Readers   **3**
For Your Health   **12**
Market Place   **30-31**
Local Events   **40-43**

CONTEST: Enter Now! **P.3**

Apples:
• *Delicious*
• *McIntosh*
• *Cortland*
• *Gala &*
  more
  on
  p.7

Katey
runs
on
Apple
Power

Oct Issue "The Right Bite"
Apple House Pub, Inc.   Harrisburg, PA.

Purpose of Text Features
Organizes Information
• table of contents • index • glossary • appendix
Signals Important Information
• titles • headings • subheadings • bold, colored, or italicized print • underlining • font • bullets
Expands Meaning of Text
• illustrations and captions • sidebar • maps • chart/tables • time line • graphs • diagrams

Text Features Found in Magazines		
Feature	**Check box if found**	**Page Number**
Table of Contents		
Glossary		
Appendix		
Index		
Title		
Heading		
Subheading		
Bold Print		
Italics		
Bullets		
Caption		
Sidebar or Inset		
Map		
Illustration or Graphics		
Chart or Table		
Diagram		

ABCs of Conducting a Survey

What Is a Survey?

A survey is a way of collecting information. Surveys are usually written, although sometimes the surveyor reads the questions aloud and writes down the answers for another person.

Types of Surveys

There are two common types of surveys: a census and a sample survey. A census involves contacting the total population of the group in which you are interested in surveying. A sample survey involves contacting only a portion of the total group in which you are interested.

Survey Question Strategy

There are several types of questions that can be used in creating a survey.

- *Open-ended*: requires more than just one- or two-word answers. These are often "how" or "why" questions. For example: "Why is it important to wear a seat belt when riding in a car?"

- *Closed-ended*: require "yes" or "no" answers. For example: "Do you always wear a seat belt when riding in a car?"

- *Multiple choice*: requires the person to select one answer from a few possible choices. For example: When I ride in a car, I wear a seat belt   a) every time   b) most times   c) sometimes   d) rarely   e) never.

- *Liker scale*: requires the person to rate items on a response scale. For example: "Rate how you feel about the following statement on a 1-to-5 response scale: It is important to wear a seat belt.   1 = strongly disagree, 2 = disagree, 3 = undecided, 4 = agree, 5 = strongly agree.

Steps in Conducting a Survey

1. Design and conduct survey
2. Organize and analyze survey data
3. Graph survey data
4. Summarize results

Name: _____ Date: _____

The Ins and Outs of Graphing

A **graph** is a visual tool that makes it easier for us to see information. Different types of graphs are appropriate for different types of information. Three common types of graphs are line, bar, and circle graphs.

Line Graph: A line graph is used to show how data changes over time. Both variables in a line graph must be numbers. The data is connected by a rising or falling line. The graph has an x-axis (horizontal) and a y-axis (vertical). Usually, the x-axis has numbers for the time period, and the y-axis has numbers for what is being measured.

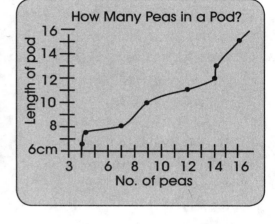

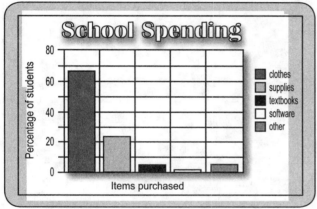

Bar Graph: A bar graph is used to compare values. The graph has an x-axis (horizontal) and a y-axis (vertical). The information is represented with horizontal or vertical bars drawn for each value.

Circle Graph: A circle graph is used to show percentages or factions of a whole. Circle graphs are sometimes called pie charts.

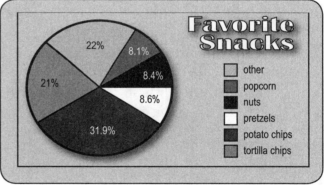

Which type of graph will you use to display your survey results? Explain why you chose this particular type of graph. _____

_____

_____

_____

_____

_____

Name: _____ Date: _____

Survey Planner

Directions: Read the "ABCs of Conducting a Survey" handout. Then complete the steps below to plan and organize your survey.

Steps

Step #1: Determine the purpose of the survey.

What do you want to find out? _____

_____

Step #2: Decide which type of survey you will use to collect your data.

Will you use a census or sample survey? _____

Step #3: Decide the method you will use to collect your data.

Will your survey be written or oral? _____

How will you distribute the survey? _____

Step #4: Create Questions

Which question strategy will you use? _____

Write the questions on the lines below. (If you need more space, write the questions on the back of this paper.)

1. _____

2. _____

3. _____

4. _____

5. _____

6. _____

7. _____

8. _____

9. _____

10. _____

Name: _____ Date: _____

Survey Planner (cont.)

Step #5: Create the Questionnaire

Use a word-processing program to create the questionnaire for the survey.

Step #6: Conduct the Survey

How will you distribute the survey?_____

How will you collect the completed surveys? _____

Step #7: Organize Data

How will you tabulate the results of the questionnaire? One way is to create a table to display the total number of responses for each question.

_____

Step #8: Graph Survey Results

Which type of graph will you use to display your data? _____

Use the information in your table to create your graph. An online site or computer program can be used to help make the graph.

Step #9: Summarize Results

Once you have your data organized and graphed, examine the numbers. What do they mean? What did you learn from the survey? Write a brief report summarizing the results of your survey.

_____

_____

_____

_____

_____

_____

_____

_____

_____

_____

_____

_____

Teacher Page

Unit: Student Plagiarism

Project Overview

Students will research plagiarism and use the information to create a multimedia presentation to share with others.

Project Objectives

When students complete this project, they will be able to write an explanatory essay and cite sources correctly. They will be able to use technology to create and share a multimedia presentation.

Integration of Academic Skills

- History/Social Studies—research examples of plagiarism
- Language Arts—write explanatory essay
- Technology—use computer word-processing and graphic programs

Primary Common Core State Standards (CCSS) Addressed:

ELA-Literacy.W.6.2 Write informative/explanatory texts to examine a topic and convey ideas, concepts, and information through the selection, organization, and analysis of relevant content.
ELA-Literacy.W.6.6 Use technology, including the Internet, to produce and publish writing as well as to interact and collaborate with others; demonstrate sufficient command of keyboarding skills to type a minimum of three pages in a single sitting.

ELA-Literacy.W.7.2 Write informative/explanatory texts to examine a topic and convey ideas, concepts, and information through the selection, organization, and analysis of relevant content.
ELA-Literacy.W.7.6 Use technology, including the Internet, to produce and publish writing and link to and cite sources as well as to interact and collaborate with others, including linking to and citing sources.

ELA-Literacy.W.8.2 Write informative/explanatory texts to examine a topic and convey ideas, concepts, and information through the selection, organization, and analysis of relevant content.
ELA-Literacy.W.8.6 Use technology, including the Internet, to produce and publish writing and present the relationships between information and ideas efficiently as well as to interact and collaborate with others.

© Copyright 2010. National Governors Association Center for Best Practices and Council of Chief State School Officers. All rights reserved.

Introductory Event

1. *Scenario:* The middle-school faculty is concerned about the amount of plagiarism found in student work.
2. *Discussion:* As a class, discuss what students know about plagiarism and copyright laws. Generate a list of what students need to know about plagiarism.
3. *Guest speaker:* Invite a community member with a background in plagiarism and copyright laws, such as a lawyer or newspaper editor, to speak to the class.

Essential Question

What can be done to stop plagiarism at our middle school?

Project Task

Research one area of concern about plagiarism and write an explanatory essay on the topic.

Product

Multimedia presentation to share recommendation for stopping plagiarism at the middle school.

Materials/Resources Needed

1. "Explanatory Writing Rubric" and "Multimedia Presentation Rubric" (assessment handout)
2. "Student Project Planner" (handout)
3. "Note Taking" (mini lesson handout)
4. "Source Cards" (mini lesson handout)
5. "How to Write an Outline" (mini lesson handout)
6. "Explanatory Writing Guide" (mini lesson handout)
7. "The Writing Process" (mini lesson handout)

Technology

Computer with word processing, presentation, and graphic programs; Internet connections; and printers.

Internet Tools for Creating a Multimedia Presentation

Animoto <http://animoto.com/education/classroom> This site turns still photos, music, and videos into video presentations.

Prezi <http://prezi.com> This site allows students to go 'outside the box' to create presentations.

BibMe <www.bibme.org> This site offers an easy-to-use automatic bibliography maker.

Managing the Project

Step 1: Activity—Launch introductory event, discuss the essential question, and generate a list of researchable questions.

Step 2: Review—"Explanatory Writing Rubric" and "Multimedia Presentation Rubric" handouts.

Step 3: Review—"Student Project Planner" handout.

Step 4: Activity—Each student writes a thesis statement stating the main idea they will develop in their explanatory essay.

Step 5: Mini lesson—"Note Taking" handout.

Step 6: Mini lesson—"Source Cards" handout.

Step 7: Students begin their research. They create source cards or use an electronic organizer. They create note cards to record relevant information that supports their thesis.

Step 8: Mini lesson—"How to Write an Outline" handout.

Step 9: Students organize their note cards and create an outline.

Step 10: Mini lesson—"Explanatory Writing Guide" handout.

Step 11: Mini lesson—"The Writing Process" handout.

Step 12: Activity—Students use a computer word-processing program to compose their explanatory essays.

Step 13: Activity—Students create multimedia presentations and share their solutions.

Project Evaluation

1. The teacher completes the "Multimedia Presentation Rubric" for each team.
2. The teacher and the students complete the "Explanatory Writing Rubric."
3. Teacher/student conferences are held to discuss the completed evaluations.

Student Project Planner

Question: What can be done to stop plagiarism at our middle school?

Project: Research one area of concern from the list generated in the introductory event dealing with plagiarism. Use the research to write an explanatory essay. Create a multimedia product to share your solutions for the problem of student plagiarism.

Steps

Step 1: Review the "Explanatory Writing Rubric" and "Multimedia Presentation Rubric" handouts.

Step 2: Formulate researchable questions in one area of concern dealing with plagiarism from the list generated by the class. Begin by listing basic questions about your topic. Focus on the *who, what, where, when,* and *why* of your topic.

Step 3: Write a thesis statement. A thesis statement is one or two sentences clearly stating the main idea that you will develop in your essay.

Step 4: Review note taking. Read the "Note Taking" and "Source Card" handouts.

Step 5: Locate and evaluate sources. Begin your research by looking for information about your topic in books, magazines, newspapers, and online. For each source, record the bibliography information on a separate index card. You will need this information for your bibliography. Record relevant evidence that supports your thesis on note cards.

Step 6: Organize notes. Sort note cards by subtopics. Evaluate each note for usefulness or need for further research. Arrange notes into a logical order for writing.

Step 7: Review the steps for writing an explanatory essay. Read the "Explanatory Writing Guide," "The Writing Process," and "How to Write an Outline" handouts.

Step 8: Create your outline. Use the outline to write your explanatory essay.

Step 9: Create a multimedia presentation. Share your presentation through the classroom Wiki, blog, or website.

Step 10: Complete the student section of the "Explanatory Writing Rubric" and "Multimedia Presentation Rubric."

Name: _____ Date: _____

Explanatory Writing Rubric

<table>
<tr><th></th><th>Student</th><th>Teacher</th><th></th></tr>
<tr><th rowspan="12">Explanatory Essay</th><th>Score</th><th>Score</th><th>Organization and Development of Ideas</th></tr>
<tr><td>4</td><td>4</td><td>Writing gives a clear and concise explanation of the problem and its significance. Presents a workable solution and includes details that explain and support it. Concludes by restating the problem.</td></tr>
<tr><td>3</td><td>3</td><td>Writing gives an explanation of the problem and its significance. Presents a solution and includes details that explain and support it. Concludes by restating the problem.</td></tr>
<tr><td>2</td><td>2</td><td>Writing presents a problem, gives a solution, and includes a conclusion.</td></tr>
<tr><td>1</td><td>1</td><td>Writing omits one or more of the explanatory essay components: problem, solution, and conclusion.</td></tr>
<tr><th>Score</th><th>Score</th><th>Use of Language/Conventions and Grammar</th></tr>
<tr><td>4</td><td>4</td><td>Word choice and language are clear, concise, and appropriate to the writing task. Correct grammar, punctuation, and spelling.</td></tr>
<tr><td>3</td><td>3</td><td>Most of the time word choice and language are clear, concise, and appropriate to the writing task. Minor errors in grammar, punctuation, and spelling.</td></tr>
<tr><td>2</td><td>2</td><td>Some of the writing is vague and confusing. Several errors in grammar, punctuation, and spelling.</td></tr>
<tr><td>1</td><td>1</td><td>Writing is vague and confusing. Errors in grammar, punctuation, and spelling interfere with the readability.</td></tr>
<tr><th rowspan="5">Sources</th><th>Score</th><th>Score</th><th>Citations</th></tr>
<tr><td>4</td><td>4</td><td>Used a variety of resources. Cited all sources of information correctly and in the proper format. Used up-to-date resources. Resources were reliable and credible.</td></tr>
<tr><td>3</td><td>3</td><td>Used a variety of resources. Cited most sources of information correctly and in the proper format. Most resources used were up-to-date, reliable, and credible.</td></tr>
<tr><td>2</td><td>2</td><td>Limited resources, incorrect citations and/or incorrect format, not all resources were current, reliable, and/or credible.</td></tr>
<tr><td>1</td><td>1</td><td>Used few resources, citations incomplete or inaccurate. Did not use the proper format. Resources were not current, reliable, and/or credible.</td></tr>
</table>

Teacher Comments: _____

_____

_____

Student Comments: _____

_____

_____

Name: _____ Date: _____

Multimedia Presentation Rubric

Student Score	Teacher Score	Appearance
4	4	Good balance of text and graphics. Words are easy to read. Titles and headings are easy to distinguish from text.
3	3	Text and graphics are balanced. Words are readable. Titles and headings are distinguishable from text.
2	2	The balance between text and graphics needs some improvement. Some print features distract from readability.
1	1	Poor use of text and graphics. Overall readability is difficult. Poor use of titles and headings.
Score	**Score**	**Multimedia (graphics, images, music, sound and/or video)**
4	4	Used multimedia components to clarify information and add interest.
3	3	Used multimedia components in presentation.
2	2	Use of multimedia components added little to presentation.
1	1	Use of multimedia components distracted from presentation.
Score	**Score**	**Content Organization**
4	4	Covers topic completely and in depth. Includes essential information: description of the problem and why it needs to be solved, recommended solution, explanation of solution, and conclusion.
3	3	Includes essential information.
2	2	Includes some essential information.
1	1	Includes little essential information.
Score	**Score**	**Mechanics**
4	4	All grammar, spelling, punctuation, and capitalization are correct.
3	3	1-2 errors in grammar, spelling, punctuation, and/or capitalization.
2	2	3-4 errors in grammar, spelling, punctuation, and/or capitalization.
1	1	5 or more errors in grammar, spelling, punctuation, and/or capitalization.

Teacher Comments: _____

_____

Student Comments: _____

_____

Note Taking

As you find information that you want to use in your essay, record each fact or detail on a separate index card. Three note-taking methods are listed below.
- *Quoting:* copying the author's exact wording or phrasing and enclosing it in quotation marks
- *Paraphrasing:* restating the main idea and supporting details of the passage in your own words
- *Summarizing:* rephrasing the main ideas of the passage

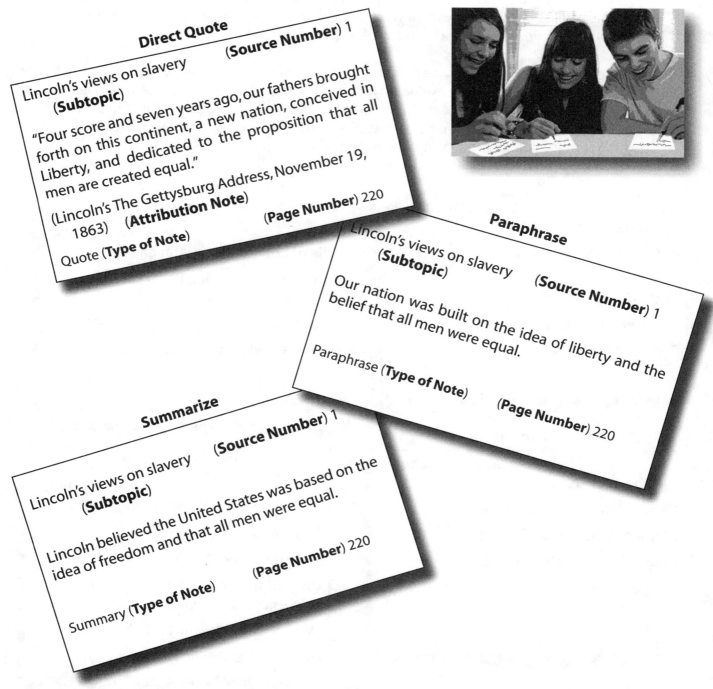

Direct Quote

Lincoln's views on slavery **(Subtopic)**   **(Source Number)** 1

"Four score and seven years ago, our fathers brought forth on this continent, a new nation, conceived in Liberty, and dedicated to the proposition that all men are created equal."

(Lincoln's The Gettysburg Address, November 19, 1863) **(Attribution Note)**

Quote **(Type of Note)**

Paraphrase

Lincoln's views on slavery **(Subtopic)**   **(Source Number)** 1

Our nation was built on the idea of liberty and the belief that all men were equal.

Paraphrase **(Type of Note)**

(Page Number) 220

Summarize

Lincoln's views on slavery   **(Source Number)** 1
(Subtopic)

Lincoln believed the United States was based on the idea of freedom and that all men were equal.

Summary **(Type of Note)**   **(Page Number)** 220

Source Cards

Step #1   **Select Sources:** Begin your research by looking for information about your topic in books, magazines, and online.

Step #2   **Evaluate Sources:**
- Check the author's credentials. Is the author an expert on the topic? Has the author written other books or articles on the topic? Has the author been published in a respected publication or on a respected website?
- Check the publication date. Is publication the most current information on your topic?
- Check reliability of the source: If you have questions about whether you are using a credible source, ask your teacher or media center specialist.

Step #3   **Create Source Cards:** Source cards are a method of recording the bibliographic information for each source you have evaluated and are going to use. The information can be recorded on index cards. Number each source card sequentially. The bibliographic information will vary depending on the type of source. The examples below show how to create a card for a book, encyclopedia, magazine, and online source.

Book

Source Number: 1

Author: Lincoln, Abraham

Title: *Lincoln: Speeches and Writings: 1861-1865*

City of Publication: New York

Publisher: Library of America

Date of Publication: 1989

Encyclopedia

Source Number: 2

Title of Entry: Lincoln, Abraham

Title of Encyclopedia: *World Book Encyclopedia*

Edition: 15th ed.

Date of Publication: 2013

Magazine

Source Number: 3

Author: Athans, Sandra K.

Title of Article: "A Historic Address"

Title of Magazine: *Cobblestone*

Date of Publication: Oct. 2008

Page Number: 22

Internet Website

Source Number: 4

Author: Freidel, Frank and Hugh Sidey

Title: "Abraham Lincoln"

Website Name: *The Presidents*

URL: <http://www.whitehouse.gov/about/presidents/abrahamlincoln>

Date of Upload: April 25, 2006

Date of Access: Nov. 12, 2013

How to Write an Outline

An outline is a plan that will help you write your essay. An outline shows the main topics that your paper will include. A Roman numeral is used to identify each main topic. Each main topic has subtopics that develop or explain the main topic. A capital letter is used to identify each subtopic.

How Can We Help Fur-Bearing Animals to Survive?

I. Threat to survival of fur-bearing animals
   A. People buying products made from animal fur
   B. Over-hunting of fur-bearing animals
   C. Loss of habitat where fur-bearing animals live

II. Three recommended solutions
   A. Protect fur-bearing animals
   B. Inform people about the problem
   C. Create conservation areas where hunting is illegal

III. Explanation of solution
   A. Create laws protecting fur-bearing animals
   B. Conservation and education programs

IV. Conclusion
   A. Products made of fur, loss of habitat, and over-hunting threaten survival of fur-bearing animals
   B. Solutions are laws and education

Guidelines for Outlining

1. Write the title of your research paper at the top of the page. Use capital letters to begin the first, last, and all important words.

2. Use Roman numerals for main topics and capital letters for subtopics. Place a period after each Roman numeral and capital letter.

3. Begin the first word in each main topic and subtopic with a capital letter.

Explanatory Writing Guide

Explanatory writing is used to convey information about a topic or to explain an idea or concept. This type of writing clearly states and analyzes a problem, then proposes a solution to the problem. There are several types of explanatory writing: compare and contrast, cause and effect, analysis-classification and problem-solution.

Problem-Solution Essay Organization

Paragraph #1: Description of problem and why it needs to be solved.

Paragraph #2: Recommended solution

Paragraph #3: Explanation of solution

Paragraph #4: Conclusion

The Writing Process

#1 PLAN

After researching your topic . . .
- Organize your note cards. Sort cards by subtopics: description of problem, recommended solution, explanation of solution, and conclusion. Read all the notes in each subtopic and put the cards in a logical order. Discard all note cards that are not usable or duplicate information on another card.
- Create a writing plan. An outline is one type of writing plan. It shows the topics and subtopics that your paper will include.

#2 DRAFT

When writing the first draft . . .
Follow your writing plan. The purpose in writing the draft is to get what you have to say down on paper. If you cannot think of how best to say something, write it down as best you can and keep on writing.
- Compose your essay. Write in sentences and paragraphs. Use your own language. Keep the audience and purpose in mind. Stay focused on the topic.

#3 REVISE

Improve your writing by asking yourself these questions:
- Do I need to add or delete details?
- Did I use a variety of sentence structures?
- Did I make clear transitions between both sentences and paragraphs?
- Did I use the appropriate word choice for my audience and purpose?

#4 EDIT

Proofread your writing for errors in . . .
- Grammar: Check for incorrect verb forms, possessive and plural nouns, homophones and homographs, and point of view.
- Punctuation: Check for correct use of commas, semi-colons, colons, and ending punctuation.
- Capitalization: Make sure the word at the beginning of each sentence and all proper nouns are capitalized.
- Spelling: Check the correct spelling of words.

#5 PUBLISH

Publish and Share
- Publish: Use technology, including the Internet, to produce your paper and bibliography.
- Share: Include multimedia components and visual displays in the presentation.

Teacher Page

Unit: Classroom Security Cameras

Project Overview

Students will individually research student rights, use of security cameras at schools, and school violence. They will take a stand on the use of security cameras in the classroom and write an argumentative essay on the topic. Working in collaborative teams, they will plan, create, and share a multimedia presentation on the topic.

Project Objectives

When students complete this project, they will be able to write an argumentative essay and cite sources correctly. Students will be able to collaborate with peers to create and share a multimedia presentation.

Integration of Academic Skills

- History/Social Studies—research student rights
- Language Arts—write argumentative essay
- Technology—use computer word-processing and graphic programs

Primary Common Core State Standards (CCSS) Addressed:

ELA-Literacy.W.6.1 Write arguments to support claims with clear reasons and relevant evidence.
ELA-Literacy.W.6.6 Use technology, including the Internet, to produce and publish writing as well as to interact and collaborate with others; demonstrate sufficient command of keyboarding skills to type a minimum of three pages in a single sitting.

CCSS.ELA-Literacy.W.7.1 Write arguments to support claims with clear reasons and relevant evidence.
ELA-Literacy.W.7.6 Use technology, including the Internet, to produce and publish writing and link to and cite sources as well as to interact and collaborate with others, including linking to and citing sources.

CCSS.ELA-Literacy.W.8.1 Write arguments to support claims with clear reasons and relevant evidence
ELA-Literacy.W.8.6 Use technology, including the Internet, to produce and publish writing and present the relationships between information and ideas efficiently as well as to interact and collaborate with others.

© Copyright 2010. National Governors Association Center for Best Practices and Council of Chief State School Officers. All rights reserved.

Introductory Event

1. *Scenario:* Nation wide, parents, teachers, and school boards are concerned about classroom violence. It has been suggested security cameras in the classroom would be a solution.
2. *Discussion:* As a class, discuss classroom violence, student rights, and security cameras. Generate a list of what middle-school students need to know about the topic.
3. *Guest speaker:* Community member with background in law such as a lawyer or law enforcement officer.

Essential Question

Should security cameras be placed in school classrooms?

Project Task

Students individually conduct research into reasons for and against security cameras in the classroom. They write an argumentative essay as either a proponent or an opponent of the issue.

Product

Students form teams with three or four other students with the same positions on the issue of security cameras in the classroom. Each team creates a multimedia presentation and posts it on the classroom Wiki, blog, or website.

Materials/Resources Needed

1. "Project Rubric" and "Project Self-Evaluation and Reflection" (assessment handouts)
2. "Student Project Planner" (handout)
3. "What Is a Multimedia Presentation?" and "Multimedia Presentation Tools" (handouts)
4. "Writing an Argumentative Essay" (activity handout)
5. "Note Taking" and "Bibliography Guide" (mini lesson handout)
6. "Argumentative Essay Planner" (activity handout)

Technology

Computer with word-processing, presentation, and graphic programs; Internet connections; and printers

Internet Tools for Creating a Multimedia Presentation

Audioboo < http://audioboo.fm/> an online site that allows students to create a simple image and five-minute audio presentation

Glogster <http://edu.glogster.com> an online site that allows students to create with text, images, graphics, music, video, and more

Managing the Project

Step 1:   Activity—Launch introductory event, discuss the essential question, and generate a list of researchable questions.

Step 2:   Review—"Project Rubric" and "Project Self-Evaluation and Reflection" handouts.

Step 3:   Review—"Student Project Planner" handout.

Step 4:   Review—"What Is a Multimedia Presentation?" (page 3) and "Multimedia Presentation Tools" (page 4) handouts.

Step 5:   Mini lesson—"Note Taking" (page 19) handout.

Step 6:   Mini lesson—"Bibliography Guide" handout.

Step 7:   Students begin their research. They create source cards or use an electronic organizer. They create note cards to record relevant information that supports their thesis.

Step 8:   Mini lesson—"Writing an Argumentative Essay" handout.

Step 9:   Activity—"Argumentative Essay Planner" handout.

Step 10: Activity—Students use a computer word-processing program to compose their argumentative essay.

Step 11: Student teams create a multimedia presentation and share on the classroom Wiki, blog or website.

Project Evaluation

1. The teacher completes the "Project Rubric" for each student.
2. Each student completes the "Project Self-Evaluation and Reflection" handout.
3. Teacher/student conferences are held to discuss the completed evaluations.

Student Project Planner

Question: Should security cameras be placed in the middle-school classrooms?

Project: Research classroom violence, student rights, and security cameras in the classroom. Take a stand on the issue. Use the research to write an argumentative essay supporting your position. With team members, create a multimedia presentation on the issue and share it with others on the classroom Wiki, blog, or website.

Steps

Step 1: Review the "Project Rubric" and "Project Self-Evaluation and Reflection" handouts.

Step 2: Formulate research questions. Begin by listing basic questions about your topic. Focus on the *who, what, where, when*, and *why* of your topic.

Step 3: Review the "Note Taking" and "Bibliography Guide" handouts.

Step 4: Locate and evaluate sources. Begin your research by looking for information about your topic in books, magazines, newspapers, and online. For each source, record the bibliographic information on a separate index card. You will need this information for your bibliography. Record relevant evidence that supports your thesis on note cards.

Step 5: As you explore the topic, consider both sides of the issue. Use the "Writing an Argumentative Essay" handout to cite evidence that supports having cameras in the classroom and evidence that supports not having cameras in the classroom. Based on the evidence, take a stand. Write a **thesis statement**. A thesis statement is one or two sentences clearly stating your opinion about cameras in the classroom.

Step 6: Organize your notes. Sort notes by subtopics. Evaluate each note for usefulness or need for further research. Arrange notes into a logical order for writing.

Step 7: Complete the "Writing an Argumentative Essay" handout.

Step 8: Compose your argumentative essay.

Step 9: Create a multimedia presentation with your team. Share the presentation through the classroom Wiki, blog, or website.

Step 10: Complete the "Project Self-Evaluation and Refection" handout.

Name: _____ Date: _____

Project Rubric

4	3	2	1	**Argumentative Essay**
				Introduces claims clearly and supports them with relevant evidence
				Acknowledges opposing claims
				Develops the topic with relevant facts and evidence
				Uses appropriate transition words to make essay flow
				Provides a conclusion that follows format for argumentative essay
				Uses correct grammar, capitalization, punctuation, and spelling
4	**3**	**2**	**1**	**Research**
				Uses relevant and credible sources
				Cites sources accurately using correct format
4	**3**	**2**	**1**	**Multimedia Component**
				Good balance of text and graphics; words are easy to read; titles and headings are easy to distinguish from text
				Uses multimedia components such as graphics, images, music, sound, and visual displays in presentation to clarify information and add interest
				Covers topic completely and in depth; includes essential information.
				Uses correct grammar, capitalization, punctuation, and spelling
4	**3**	**2**	**1**	**Presentation**
				Correctly posted project on classroom Wiki, blog, or website.
				Covers topic completely and in depth; includes essential information
				Uses correct grammar, capitalization, punctuation, and spelling

Teacher Comments: _____

_____

_____

_____

_____

Name: _____ Date: _____

Project Self-Evaluation and Reflection

Project Title: _____

Essential Question: _____

Team Members: _____

Summarize your project.

Describe your contribution to the project.

On the next project, what would you do differently to improve your work? Explain, using examples and details.

What challenges did your team face working on the project? Explain, using examples and details.

What did you like best about the project? Explain, using examples and details.

Bibliography Guide

Sources used in a project should be compiled into a list called a bibliography or a works cited list. Use the sample entries below as a guide for writing your bibliography.

Just a Reminder . . .

Punctuate titles
Double space between entries
Allow 1-inch margin all around
Single space after punctuation marks
Font size is 10 or 12 point

Font type is Times New Roman or Arial
Entry begins against the left margin
Indent five spaces on the second line and
all following lines that belong to the entry

Examples of Bibliography Entries	
Book	**Internet Website**
Last name, First name. *Title of book*. Place of publication: Publisher, Publication Date.	Last name, First name. "Title of Item." *Website Title*. Publisher of Website, Publication Date. Medium Accessed. Date Accessed. <electronic address>.
Magazine or Newspaper Article	**Audiovisual Materials**
Last name, First name. "Title or Headline of Article." *Name of Magazine or Newspaper*. Publication Date, Page Numbers.	"Title of Material." Type of Material. Place of Publication; Publisher, Publication Date.
Signed Encyclopedia Article	**Unsigned Encyclopedia Article**
Last name, First name. "Title of Article." *Name of Encyclopedia*. Publication Date. Volume Number, Page Numbers.	"Title of Article." *Name of Encyclopedia*. Publication Date. Volume Number, Page Numbers.
CD-ROM	**Interview**
"Title of Article." *Title of CD-ROM*. Medium Accessed. Volume number. Place of Publication: Publisher, Publication Date.	Last name of person interviewed, First name of person interviewed. Type of Interview. Date.
Photographs, Illustrations, and Drawings	
Creator's Last name, First name. *Title of Photograph*. Original Publication Date. *Title of Online Collection*. Date of Posting. Current Location of Original Document. Medium Accessed. Sponsoring Organization. Date Accessed. <electronic address>.	

Name: _____   Date: _____

Writing an Argumentative Essay

In an argumentative essay, the writer makes a claim and supports it with evidence in order to convince or persuade the audience to agree. This type of easy includes three parts: **introduction**, **body**, and **conclusion**. For an argumentative essay to be effective, each part must contain certain elements. The first paragraph should include a brief explanation of your topic, background information, and claim or thesis statement. The **thesis statement** is your position on the topic. The three paragraphs of the body contain information that supports the claim with evidence and acknowledges opposing viewpoints. The conclusion restates your position.

Directions: As you explore the topic, consider both sides of the issue. List arguments for both sides of the issue in the boxes. Then write your thesis statement below.

Question: Should security cameras be used in the classroom?

Arguments For Security Cameras	**Arguments Against Security Cameras**

Thesis Statement: _____

_____

_____

Name: _____ Date: _____

Argumentative Essay Planner

Paragraph #1—Introduction

Topic: _____

Opponents believe: _____

Proponents argue: _____

Thesis Statement: (Your opinion and why) _____

_____

Paragraph #2—Claim

Claim #1: (Why someone should agree with your opinion): _____

_____

Cite evidence: (source) _____

_____

Paragraph #3—Claim

Claim #2: (Why someone should agree with your opinion): _____

_____

Cite evidence: (source) _____

_____

Paragraph #4—Claim

Claim #3: (Why someone should agree with your opinion): _____

_____

Cite evidence: (source) _____

_____

Paragraph #5—Conclusion

Restate Opponent's view: _____

_____

Restate Proponent's view: _____

_____

Restate 3 reasons you agree: _____

_____

State why your thesis statement is correct: _____

_____

Teacher Page

Unit: World War II Veterans

Project Overview

Students will videotape an interview with a World War II veteran. The class will create a Power-Point™ presentation to present at a Veterans Day Assembly. Students will submit veterans' interviews and collections to the online Veterans History Project (Library of Congress) Website.

Project Objectives

When students complete this project, they will be able to conduct an interview. Students will be able to collaborate with peers to create and share a multimedia presentation.

Integration of Academic Skills

- Language Arts—read information about the Veterans History Project and instructions for student participation in the program.
- Technology—use audio or video equipment and external microphone for interview
- Social Studies—World War II research

Primary Common Core State Standards (CCSS) Addressed:

ELA-Literacy.W.6.8 Gather relevant information from multiple print and digital sources; assess the credibility of each source; and quote or paraphrase the data and conclusions of others while avoiding plagiarism and providing basic bibliographic information for sources.

ELA-Literacy.W.6.6 Use technology, including the Internet, to produce and publish writing as well as to interact and collaborate with others; demonstrate sufficient command of keyboarding skills to type a minimum of three pages in a single sitting.

ELA-Literacy.W.7.8 Gather relevant information from multiple print and digital sources, using search terms effectively; assess the credibility and accuracy of each source; and quote or paraphrase the data and conclusions of others while avoiding plagiarism and following a standard format for citation.

ELA-Literacy.W.7.6 Use technology, including the Internet, to produce and publish writing and link to and cite sources as well as to interact and collaborate with others, including linking to and citing sources.

ELA-Literacy.W.8.8 Gather relevant information from multiple print and digital sources, using search terms effectively; assess the credibility and accuracy of each source; and quote or paraphrase the data and conclusions of others while avoiding plagiarism and following a standard format for citation.

ELA-Literacy.W.8.6 Use technology, including the Internet, to produce and publish writing and present the relationships between information and ideas efficiently as well as to interact and collaborate with others.

Introductory Event

Activity: The teacher uses a Smartboard to present a virtual tour of the Veterans History Project website and share the featured World War II veteran's interview at the Veterans History Project (Library of Congress) at <http://www.loc.gov/vets>.

Essential Question

How can students preserve oral histories of World War II veterans living in their communities?

Project Task

Interview a World War II veteran. Submit the interview to the Veterans History Project.

Product

Create a slide to be included in a class PowerPoint™ presentation to be presented at an assembly honoring veterans.

Materials/Resources Needed

1. Veterans History Project (Library of Congress) at <http://www.loc.gov/vets>
2. World War II veterans (community members)
3. "Student Project Planner" (handout)
4. "Exploring the Veterans History Project Website" (activity handout)
5. "Steps in the Veterans History Project" (activity handout)
6. "Veterans Service Research" (activity handout)
7. "Source Cards" (mini lesson handout; page 22 from the Student Plagiarism unit)
8. "Interview Outline" (activity handout) and "Basic Interview Tips" (mini lesson)
9. "Planning your PowerPoint™ Slide" (activity handout)

Technology

Computer with word-processing, presentation, and graphic programs; Internet connections; and printers.

Internet Tools for Creating a Multimedia Presentation

Animoto <http://animoto.com/education/classroom> This site turns still photos, music, and videos into video presentations.

Managing the Project

Step 1: Teacher Preparation—Review the Veterans History Project website. Go to the "Especially for Educators" page under the "How to Participate" section at <http://www.loc.gov/vets/youth-resources.html> for information, sample interviews, and interview questions.

Step 2: Activity—Launch introductory event, discuss the essential question, and present project task and required product.

Step 3: Activity—Divide students into small collaborative teams to complete the project.

Step 4: Review—"Student Project Planner," "Veterans History Project Rubric," and "Project Self-Evaluation and Reflection" handouts.

Step 5: Activity—"Exploring the Veterans History Project Website" handout

Step 6: Activity—Students print the Veterans History Project Field Kit available on the Veterans History project website. Students highlight important steps in the process and complete the "Steps in the Veterans History Project" handout.

Step 7: Activity—Students select and contact a veteran to interview. They fill out the biographical data form and release forms with the veteran and set up an interview time.

Step 8: Mini Lesson—"Source Cards" handout

Step 9: Activity—"Veterans Service Research" handout

Step 10: Activity—"Interview Outline" handout

Step 11: Mini Lesson—"Basic Interview Tips"

Step 12: Activity—Teams submit their interviews to the Veterans History Project.

Step 13: Activity—Complete the "Planning Your PowerPoint™ Slide" handout.

Step 14: Activity—Organize slides into a PowerPoint™ slideshow for a Veterans Day Assembly.

Project Evaluation

1. The teacher completes the "Veterans History Project Rubric" for each team.
2. Each student completes the "Project Self-Evaluation and Reflection" handout.
3. Teacher/student conferences are held to discuss the completed evaluations.

Student Project Planner

Question: How can students preserve oral histories of World War II veterans living in their communities?

Project: Interview a World War II veteran. Submit veterans' stories and collections to the Veterans History Project. Use the interview information to create a PowerPoint™ slide. The slide will be part of a PowerPoint™ slideshow presented at an assembly honoring World War II veterans.

Steps

Step 1: Review the "Veterans History Project Rubric" and "Project Self-Evaluation and Reflection" handouts.

Step 2: Preview the Veterans History Project at <http://www.loc.gov/vets>. Complete the "Exploring the Veterans History Project Website" handout.

Step 3: Review the steps in the project. Print the Veterans History Project Field Kit and review the guidelines of the project. Highlight important steps in the process and complete the "Steps in the Veterans History Project" handout.

Step 4: Contact a veteran to interview. Meet with the veteran to plan the interview and fill out the biographical data form and release forms.

Step 5: Review the mini lesson—"Source Cards" handout

Step 6: Prepare for the interview. Review the "Basic Interview Tips" handout. Complete the "Interview Outline" and "Veterans Service Research" handouts.

Step 7: Conduct and record the interview.

Step 8: Submit the interview to the Veterans History Project.

Step 9: Create a biographical PowerPoint™ slide of the veteran interviewed. Complete the "Planning Your PowerPoint™ Slide" handout.

Step 10: As a class, organize all the slides into one PowerPoint™ slideshow and present it at the Veterans Day Assembly.

Step 11: Complete the "Project Self-Evaluation and Reflection" handout.

Name: _____ Date: _____

Veterans History Project Rubric

Project Components	Below Proficiency 1	Nearing Proficient 2	Proficient 3	Advanced 4
Team Collaboration	Does not cooperate with team members or perform duties assigned to the team.	Cooperates with team members some of the time and performs some duties assigned to the team.	Cooperates with team members most of the time and performs nearly all duties assigned to the team.	Cooperates with team members and performs all duties assigned to the team.
Research	Extracted a lot of information that wasn't relevant.	Extracted some relevant information.	Extracted mostly relevant information.	Extracted relevant information.
Citations	Citations were incomplete or inaccurate.	Cited some sources of information in proper format.	Cited most sources of information in proper format.	Cited all sources of information accurately.
Interview Questions	Few questions were designed to draw out information from person interviewed.	Some questions were designed to draw out information from person interviewed.	Most questions were designed to draw out information from person interviewed.	Questions were designed to draw out information from person interviewed.
Interview	Presentation was disjointed and interest level was low.	Majority of presentation was disjointed and interest level was low.	Majority of the presentation flowed and was interesting.	Presentation flowed well, kept the attention of the audience, and was very interesting.
PowerPoint™ Slide	Incomplete	Some slide criteria met.	Most slide criteria met.	All criteria met

Teacher Comments: _____

_____

_____

_____

_____

Name: _____ Date: _____

Project Self-Evaluation and Reflection

1. Write a brief summary of the Veterans History Project.

   _____

   _____

   _____

   _____

2. Did your World War II research help you with the interview? Explain, using two examples to support your answer. _____

   _____

   _____

   _____

3. What are a few things you learned while working on the project?

   _____

   _____

   _____

   _____

4. What did you like best and least about your final project? Cite examples and details to support your answer. _____

   _____

   _____

   _____

5. How did the project make you feel after completion? Explain.

   _____

   _____

   _____

   _____

6. How would you rate your work on the project (Excellent / Good / Fair / Poor)? Explain. _____

   _____

   _____

Name: _____ Date: _____

Exploring the Veterans History Project Website

Directions: Explore the Veterans History Project Website at the Library of Congress. There are five headings on the Web page. Write a brief summary of the information for each heading in the graphic organizer.

Title: *Veterans History Project*
Source: The Library of Congress
<http://www.loc.gov/vets/vets-home.html>

Headings	Summary
About the Project	
How to Participate	
Search the Veterans Collection	
Frequently Asked Questions	
News and Events	

39

Name: _____ Date: _____

Steps in the Veterans History Project

Directions: Learn about the Veterans History Project at the Library of Congress. Download the Veterans History Project Field Guide. There are five steps to the project. Write the name of the step in the first column of the graphic organizer. In the second column, summarize the step.

> **Title**: *Veterans History Project*
> **Source**: The Library of Congress
> <http://www.loc.gov/vets/vets-home.html>

Steps to Follow	Summary
Step 1	
Step 2	
Step 3	
Step 4	
Step 5	

Name: _____ Date: _____

Veterans Service Research

Directions: Through your initial contact with the veteran, you learned the role the person played during World War II. Now it's time to do some research about the war to be better prepared for your interview. Begin your research by looking for information in books, magazines, newspapers, and online. Choose three sources you will use. Read and summarize the information, and record the bibliography information.

Source 1: Summary
_____
_____
_____
_____

Citation
_____
_____

Source 2: Summary
_____
_____
_____
_____

Citation
_____
_____

Source 3: Summary
_____
_____
_____
_____

Citation
_____
_____

Name: _____ Date: _____

Interview Outline

Directions: Fill in the outline below with questions that you would like to ask the veteran. (See Step 3 "The Interview" located in the Project Field Kit.)

I. Biographical Details

    A. _____

    B. _____

    C. _____

II. Early Service Days

    A. _____

    B. _____

    C. _____

    D. _____

III. Wartime Service

    A. _____

    B. _____

    C. _____

    D. _____

IV. Coming Home

    A. _____

    B. _____

    C. _____

    D. _____

V. Reflections

    A. _____

    B. _____

    C. _____

    D. _____

Basic Interview Tips

Tip 1:   Contact the person to be interviewed and explain who you are, why you want to talk to him or her, and what you wish to find out.

Tip 2:   Be polite.

Tip 3:   Set a time to conduct the interview.

Tip 4:   Let the veteran know approximately how long the interview will last.

Tip 5:   Prepare for the interview by finding out some background information about the interviewee.

Tip 6:   Prepare specific questions and never ask questions that can be answered with "yes" or "no."

Tip 7:   Be prepared for the interview. Bring a pencil, notebook, interview questions, and a recording device. (Before the interview starts, obtain permission to use a recording device.)

Tip 8:   Dress neatly to let the interviewee know that you are serious about the interview.

Tip 9:   Maintain eye contact when asking questions.

Tip 10:   Don't interrupt. Keep your own comments to a minimum.

Tip 11:   Listen carefully to the answers given. The answer could lead to other questions. Don't ask a question that has already been answered.

Tip 12:   Conduct your interview like a conversation. Don't be afraid to ask about things you don't understand. Let the interview take a natural flow.

Tip 13:   Remember to thank your interviewee and leave him or her with your school contact information.

Name: _____ Date: _____

Planning Your PowerPoint™ Slide

Directions: Design and create one PowerPoint™ slide that will honor the veteran you interviewed. Each team member will create a slide, and then the team will select the best one to use in the presentation at the Veterans Day assembly. (If there is enough time, all slides may be used in the presentation.) This slide will be used along with your classmates' slides to produce one PowerPoint™ presentation. Fill in the planner and have required information written and proofed before you log in on a computer.

Slide Information

Veteran's Name: _____

Veteran's Photograph? (circle one)   Yes   No

Dates of Service: _____

Branch of the Military: _____

Where was the veteran stationed during the war? _____

_____

In which war event did the veteran participate? _____

_____

Other slide considerations:

    text font and color: _____

    background color: _____

    slide transitions: _____

    custom animations: _____

Working as a team, prepare a 30- to 45-second "Thank You" script that will go along with the slide. The script could reflect how proud you are or perhaps highlight a few things learned from this experience.

    •   The script could be read (performed) by your team at the assembly.

                OR

    •   Use Animoto, an online site, to create a PowerPoint™ presentation. This site will allow you to add voice to your slide.

Teacher Page

Unit: Folklife

Project Overview

Students collaborate with peers to collect information about the traditional heritage of their community. Students submit collections to the online American Folklife Center (Library of Congress) Website. They share their research findings with the community through museum exhibits.

Project Objectives

When students complete this project, they will be able to conduct an interview. Students will be able to collaborate with peers to create and share a multimedia presentation.

Integration of Academic Skills

- Language Arts—read website information about the American Folklife Center
- Technology—use digital cameras, video equipment, and computer word processing
- Social Studies—learn historical information through community-based collaboration

Primary Common Core State Standards (CCSS) Addressed:

ELA-Literacy.W.6.8 Gather relevant information from multiple print and digital sources; assess the credibility of each source; and quote or paraphrase the data and conclusions of others while avoiding plagiarism and providing basic bibliographic information for sources.
ELA-Literacy.W.6.6 Use technology, including the Internet, to produce and publish writing as well as to interact and collaborate with others; demonstrate sufficient command of keyboarding skills to type a minimum of three pages in a single sitting.

ELA-Literacy.W.7.8 Gather relevant information from multiple print and digital sources, using search terms effectively; assess the credibility and accuracy of each source; and quote or paraphrase the data and conclusions of others while avoiding plagiarism and following a standard format for citation.
ELA-Literacy.W.7.6 Use technology, including the Internet, to produce and publish writing and link to and cite sources as well as to interact and collaborate with others, including linking to and citing sources.

ELA-Literacy.W.8.8 Gather relevant information from multiple print and digital sources, using search terms effectively; assess the credibility and accuracy of each source; and quote or paraphrase the data and conclusions of others while avoiding plagiarism and following a standard format for citation.
ELA-Literacy.W.8.6 Use technology, including the Internet, to produce and publish writing and present the relationships between information and ideas efficiently as well as to interact and collaborate with others.

© Copyright 2010. National Governors Association Center for Best Practices and Council of Chief State School Officers. All rights reserved.

Introductory Event

Activity: The teacher uses a Smartboard to share historical collections from the American Folklife Center (Library of Congress) Website at <http://www.loc.gov/folklife>.
Discussion: As a class, discuss the cultural heritage of the community.

Essential Question

How can students preserve and share the cultural heritage of their community?

Project Task

Conduct fieldwork to collect information about the traditional heritage of the community. Submit the collection to the American Folklife Center for preservation.

Product

Museum exhibit presenting cultural heritage of their community.

Materials/Resources Needed

1. American Folklife Center <http://www.loc.gov/folklife>
2. Community members
3. "Folklife Exhibit Project Rubric" and "Peer Evaluation" (assessment handouts)
4. "Student Project Planner" (handout)
5. *Folklife and Fieldwork* booklet (download at <http://www.loc.gov/folklife/fieldwork>)
6. "Folklife and Fieldwork" (activity handout)
7. "Note Taking," "Source Cards" (handouts from pages 21–22 from Student Plagiarism unit)
8. "Documentation and Interview Planner" (activity handout)
9. "Basic Interview Tips" (mini lesson handout; page 43 from the World War II Veterans unit)
10. "What Does a Museum Exhibit Look Like?" (activity handout)
11. "Museum Exhibit Rules and Guidelines" (handout)
12. "Folklife Museum Exhibit Planner" (activity handout)
13. Artifacts for the exhibition; tri-fold display board, art supplies

Technology

Computer with word-processing, presentation, and graphic programs; Internet connections; and printers

Internet Tools for Creating a Multimedia Presentation

Animoto <http://animoto.com/education/classroom> This site turns still photos, music, and videos into video presentations.

BibMe <www.bibme.org> This site offers an easy-to-use automatic bibliography maker.

Managing the Project

Step 1: Activity—Launch introductory event, discuss the essential question, and present project task and required product.
Step 2: Activity—Divide students into collaborative teams to complete the project.
Step 3: Review—"Student Project Planner," "Folklife Exhibit Project Rubric," and "Peer Evaluation" handouts.
Step 4: Activity—Students download *Folklife and Fieldwork* booklet from <http://www.loc.gov/folklife/fieldwork/pdf/fieldwkComplete.pdf> and complete the "Folklife and Fieldwork" handout.
Step 5: Activity—Students select a folklife topic and "tradition-bearer."
Step 6: Mini Lesson—"Note Taking" and "Source Cards" handouts.
Step 7: Activity—Students research their folklife topic.
Step 8: Activity—"Documentation and Interview Planner" handout.
Step 9: Activity—Review "Basic Interview Tips" handout. Students conduct interview.
Step 10: Activity—Students submit their folklife project to the American Folklife Center.
Step 11: Review—"What Does a Museum Exhibit Look Like?" and "Museum Rules and Guidelines" handouts.
Step 12: Activity—"Folklife Museum Exhibit Planner" handout.
Step 13: Activity—Student teams create a museum exhibit and share with the community.

Project Evaluation

1. The teacher completes the "Folklife Exhibit Project Rubric" for each team.
2. For each exhibit, student completes the "Peer Evaluation" handout.
3. Teacher/student conferences are held to discuss the completed evaluations.

Student Project Planner

Question: How can students share and preserve the cultural heritage of their community?

Project: Collaborate with peers to collect information about the traditional heritage of your community. Submit the information to the online American Folklife Center (Library of Congress) Website. Create a museum exhibit to share the information with your community.

Steps

Step 1: Review the "Folklife Exhibit Project Rubric" and "Peer Evaluation" handouts.

Step 2: Print and read the Folklife and Fieldwork booklet from <http://www.loc.gov/folklife/fieldwork/pdf/fieldwkComplete.pdf>.

Step 3: Complete the "Folklife and Fieldwork" handout.

Step 4: Select a folklife topic and "tradition-bearer." (See page 7 of the *Folklife and Fieldwork* booklet.)

Step 5: Review note taking. Read the "Note Taking" and "Source Card" handouts.

Step 6: Locate and evaluate sources. Look for information about your topic in books, magazines, newspapers, and online. For each source, record the bibliography information on a separate index card. You will need this information for your bibliography. Record relevant information on note cards.

Step 7: Meet with the "tradition-bearer" to plan the interview and fill out the release form. (See Step 36 of the *Folklife and Fieldwork* booklet.)

Step 8: Prepare for interview. Review the "Basic Interview Tips" handout and complete the "Documentation and Interview Planner" handout.

Step 9: Conduct and record the interview.

Step 10: Submit the interview to the American Folklife Center. (See page 19 of the *Folklife and Fieldwork* booklet.)

Step 11: Create a museum exhibit using your research and interview information. Review the "Museum Exhibit Rules and Guidelines" handout and complete the "What Does a Museum Exhibit Look Like?" and "Folklife Museum Exhibit Planner" handouts.

Step 12: Open the museum to the community.

Step 13: Complete the "Peer Evaluation" handout.

Name: _____ Date: _____

Folklife Exhibit Project Rubric

Project Components	Below Proficiency 1	Nearing Proficient 2	Proficient 3	Advanced 4
Engaging and Interesting	Exhibit is not interesting or engaging.	Exhibit contains some parts that are interesting and engaging.	Most of the exhibit contains parts that are interesting and engaging.	All of the exhibit is very interesting and engaging.
Visually Balanced and Attractive	Exhibit is unbalanced, unattractive, messy, and disorganized.	Exhibit is acceptably attractive and balanced, but messy and disorganized.	Exhibit is somewhat balanced and attractive, but parts are messy and disorganized.	Exhibit is well-balanced, attractive, carefully prepared, and organized effectively.
Collaborative	Participation in project was minimal.	Did the exhibit, but not interested and at times lost focus.	Used time pretty well. Stayed focused most of the time to produce exhibit.	Used time effectively in class and focused on the exhibit project.
Informative	No significant facts about the topic are provided.	Information about the topic is mistaken or missing.	Most of the topic is explained	The topic is well explained.
Mechanics	5 or more errors in spelling, capitalization, and/or grammar, which are distracting.	3–5 errors in spelling, capitalization, and/or grammar, which are distracting.	1–2 errors in spelling, capitalization, and/or grammar but not distracting.	No errors in spelling, capitalization, and/or grammar.

Teacher Comments: _____

_____

_____

_____

_____

Name: _____ Date: _____

Peer Evaluation

Directions: Tour the museum and evaluate the exhibits. Complete one "Peer Evaluation" for each exhibit. (You will need several copies of this handout.)

Peer Evaluation		
Name of Exhibit	**Rate the exhibit on the following; 1 (low) to 5 (high). Circle your response.**	**Favorite Part**
	Informative 1 2 3 4 5	**Area for Improvement**
	Interesting 1 2 3 4 5	
	Attractive 1 2 3 4 5	
	Organization 1 2 3 4 5	**Comments**
	Easy to Understand 1 2 3 4 5	

Peer Evaluation		
Name of Exhibit	**Rate the exhibit on the following; 1 (low) to 5 (high). Circle your response.**	**Favorite Part**
	Informative 1 2 3 4 5	**Area for Improvement**
	Interesting 1 2 3 4 5	
	Attractive 1 2 3 4 5	
	Organization 1 2 3 4 5	**Comments**
	Easy to Understand 1 2 3 4 5	

Peer Evaluation		
Name of Exhibit	**Rate the exhibit on the following; 1 (low) to 5 (high). Circle your response.**	**Favorite Part**
	Informative 1 2 3 4 5	**Area for Improvement**
	Interesting 1 2 3 4 5	
	Attractive 1 2 3 4 5	
	Organization 1 2 3 4 5	**Comments**
	Easy to Understand 1 2 3 4 5	

Name: _____ Date: _____

Folklife and Fieldwork

> **Title:** *Folklife And Fieldwork: An Introduction to Field Techniques*
> **Source:** Library of Congress, The American Folklife Center
> <http://www.loc.gov/folklife/fieldwork/pdf/fieldwkComplete.pdf>

Directions: Go to the URL address above and print the 46-page *Folklife and Fieldwork* booklet for your team. Use the booklet to answer the questions below.

1. Congress created the American Folklife Center in 1976. How does the law define *folklife*? (page 1)

    _____

    _____

    _____

2. It is helpful to think of a field project in three parts. What are the three parts? (page 3)

    _____

    _____

    _____

3. What is a "tradition-bearer"? (page 7)

    _____

    _____

    _____

4. What are some basic supplies and preparation before doing fieldwork? (page 9)

    _____

    _____

    _____

5. What is a release form? Why are they important? (page 17)

    _____

    _____

    _____

6. List four folklife topics. (pages 4–6)

    _____

    _____

    _____

Name: _____ Date: _____

Documentation and Interview Planner

Directions: Prepare for your interview by completing this page.

1. Folklife topic _____

2. Name of "tradition-bearer" _____

   The "tradition-bearer" is someone who can provide information about the folklife subject you selected to research. (See page 7 of the *Folklife and Fieldwork* booklet.)

3. Briefly tell about your "tradition-bearer."

   _____

   _____

   _____

   _____

   _____

4. List the equipment you will need to document the interview.

   _____

   _____

5. Ask yourself...

   • Have I filled out the Fieldwork Data Sheet? (See pages 29–31 of the *Folklife and Fieldwork* booklet.)

   • Do I need an audio and video log? (See page 32 of *Folklife and Fieldwork* booklet.)

   • Do I need a photo log? (See page 34 of *Folklife and Fieldwork* booklet.)

   • Do I have a release form to be signed prior to the interview? (See page 36 of *Folklife and Fieldwork* booklet.)

6. Write five questions about your folklife topic you would like to ask the "tradition-bearer."

   _____

   _____

   _____

   _____

   _____

   _____

   _____

Name: _____ Date: _____

What Does a Museum Exhibit Look Like?

> **Title:** *Panoramic Virtual Tour*
> **Source:** Smithsonian Institute
> <http://www.mnh.si.edu/panoramas/>

Directions: Think about how exhibits impart information to visitors. Complete the questionnaire while touring the Smithsonian National Museum of Natural History at the URL above.

Museum Questionnaire
Do the exhibits seem to be effective at presenting information to visitors? Explain, citing two examples.
Is there something you like or dislike about the exhibits? Support your answer with at least two details.
How are the objects positioned? Support your answer with at least two details.
Are the exhibit artifacts protected from damage? Explain, citing two examples.
Are there other ways to protect artifacts? Support your answer with at least two details.
Does lighting play a role in the exhibit? Support your answer with at least two details.

Museum Exhibit Rules and Guidelines

Directions: Read the rules and guidelines below before planning your museum exhibit. To learn more about what goes into creating a museum exhibit, go online to Chicago History Fair at < http://www.chicagohistoryfair.org/making-history/the-final-product/exhibit.html>.

Rules

- The topic must be connected to community folklife.
- All team members must be involved in the research and interpretation of the team's topic.
- Potentially dangerous items, such as weapons, guns, animals, etc., are forbidden.
- Use no more than 1,000 words for the project exhibit.
- Media devices may be used in your exhibit, but they must be able to be controlled by the visitor. The device should not run for more than four minutes.

WOOL: From Sheep to Chic

1. A sheep's coat is wool.
2. Shearing removes the wool
3. Next, the wool is cleaned
4. Wool is carded into strands
5. Strands are spun into yarn on a spinning wheel
6. Yarn is woven into cloth on a loom.
7. Cloth is made into clothing and other items.

In preindustrial times, looms were kept in homes or by small merchants. The Industrial Age gave rise to huge factories to take over the labor-intensive work of turning wool into cloth. Child labor was a sad reality in this industry.

Basic Guidelines

- The exhibit must be neatly presented on a tri-fold display (must be free standing); the entire exhibit should not exceed 6 feet tall by 4 feet wide by 3 feet deep.
- The exhibit must include a brief summary of your folklife topic. Use your research and interview to write the summary.
- Select fonts that reflect your folklife topic. Use different font sizes based on the importance of text: consider using larger fonts (48+ pt.) for title and subtitles. Select readable styles and type for labels: 24–28 pt. font size.
- Present your information clearly and in an organized manner to avoid clutter.
- Your design delivers your message; connect content to your design. Create a visual design and layout that will reinforce the message.
- Choose colors that reflect your topic. Try using different color background mats for different parts and sections of your exhibit.
- The title sends your message; craft a catchy title that is also informative.
- The majority of your sections will include subtitles, labels, and primary and secondary sources.
- Select the most important artifacts for your exhibit.

Name: _____   Date: _____

Folklife Museum Exhibit Planner

Directions: Plan and sketch your exhibit layout before you begin creating the full-scale project. Include your research. Decide which photos, charts, maps, or other visuals provide support to your topic. Remember to put your title in the largest font. Labels and captions need to be readable to the viewer.

Title:
Design and Color Ideas:
Subtitles for each section of your exhibit: • • • • •

Sketch It Out

Teacher Page

Unit: Dust Bowl

Project Overview

Students will research the causes and consequences of the Dust Bowl. They will select a photograph about this event from the American Memory Collection on the Library of Congress Website. They will write a newspaper article using their research and photograph. Students will post the article on the classroom Wiki, blog, or website.

Project Objectives

When students complete this project, they will be able to write a newspaper article. They will be able to use technology to create and share the article.

Integration of Academic Skills

- Language Arts—write a newspaper article
- Technology—use a computer to write and share a newspaper article
- Social Studies—research the Dust Bowl topic

Primary Common Core State Standards (CCSS) Addressed:

ELA-Literacy.W.6.2 Write informative/explanatory texts to examine a topic and convey ideas, concepts, and information through the selection, organization, and analysis of relevant content.	ELA-Literacy.W.7.2 Write informative/explanatory texts to examine a topic and convey ideas, concepts, and information through the selection, organization, and analysis of relevant content.	ELA-Literacy.W.8.2 Write informative/explanatory texts to examine a topic and convey ideas, concepts, and information through the selection, organization, and analysis of relevant content.
ELA-Literacy.W.6.6 Use technology, including the Internet, to produce and publish writing as well as to interact and collaborate with others; demonstrate sufficient command of keyboarding skills to type a minimum of three pages in a single sitting.	ELA-Literacy.W.7.6 Use technology, including the Internet, to produce and publish writing and link to and cite sources as well as to interact and collaborate with others, including linking to and citing sources.	ELA-Literacy.W.8.6 Use technology, including the Internet, to produce and publish writing and present the relationships between information and ideas efficiently as well as to interact and collaborate with others.

© Copyright 2010. National Governors Association Center for Best Practices and Council of Chief State School Officers. All rights reserved.

Introductory Event

1. *Activity:* The teacher uses a Smartboard to share photographs of the Dust Bowl era from the American Memory Collections (Library of Congress) website at <http://memory.loc.gov/ammem/index.html>.
2. *Discussion:* As a class, discuss what students know about the Dust Bowl.
3. *Video*: View one of several Dust Bowl videos available on the Public Broadcasting Service Website at < http://video.pbs.org/program/dust-bowl/>.
4. *Text Mapping:* Students identify informational text features found in newspapers. They use different colored markers to highlight, circle, or otherwise mark the different text features they locate. Page 10 from the Student Handbook unit can also be used as a review.
5. *Discussion:* Display a variety of primary sources, including photographs. Define primary sources and secondary sources.

Essential Question

What was it like for people living through the Dust Bowl era?

Project Task

Write a newspaper article identifying the causes and consequences of the Dust Bowl.

Product

Create a multimedia presentation and post it on the classroom Wiki, blog or website.

Materials/Resources Needed

1. "Newspaper Article Project Rubric" (assessment handouts)
2. American Memory Collection (Library of Congress) <http://memory.loc.gov/ammem/index.html>
3. "Student Project Planner" (handout)
4. "Bibliography Guide" (mini lesson handout; page 31 from the Classroom Security Cameras unit)
5. "Dust Bowl Research" (activity handout)
6. "Primary Source: Photograph Analysis" (activity handout)
7. "Writing a Newspaper Article" (mini lesson handout)
8. "Newspaper Article Planner" (activity handout)

Technology

Computer with word-processing, presentation, and graphic programs; Internet connections; and printers

Internet Tools for Creating a Multimedia Presentation

BibMe <www.bibme.org> This site offers an easy-to-use automatic bibliography maker.

Managing the Project

Step 1: Activity—Launch introductory event, discuss the essential question, and present project task and required product.

Step 2: Activity—Review the "Newspaper Article Project Rubric" handout.

Step 3: Review—"Student Project Planner" handout.

Step 4: Mini Lesson—"Bibliography Guide" handout.

Step 5: Activity—Students research the causes and consequences of the Dust Bowl. Students complete the "Dust Bowl Research" and "Primary Source: Photograph Analysis" handouts.

Step 6: Mini Lesson—"Writing a Newspaper Article" handout.

Step 7: Activity—Students plan their article using the "Newspaper Article Planner" handout.

Step 8: Activity—Students share their project by posting their newspaper article on the classroom Wiki, blog, or website.

Project Evaluation

1. The teacher and students complete the "Newspaper Article Project Rubric."
2. Teacher/student conferences are held to discuss the completed evaluations.

Student Project Planner

Question: What was it like for people living through the Dust Bowl era?

Project: Write a newspaper article based on a historic Dust Bowl photograph. Conduct research to learn about the Dust Bowl era. Write a newspaper article reflecting on the photograph and information you collected during your research.

Steps

Step 1: Review the "Newspaper Article Project Rubric" handout.

Step 2: Review the "Bibliography Guide" handout.

Step 3: Locate and evaluate sources to complete the "Dust Bowl Research" handout. Begin your research in the library looking for information in encyclopedias, books, or the Internet.

Step 4: Go online to the American Memory Collection at the Library of Congress <http://memory.loc.gov/ammem/index.html>. Select a Dust Bowl photograph and complete the "Primary Source: Photograph Analysis" handout. The photo you selected will be included in your newspaper article.

Step 5: Review the "Writing a Newspaper Article" handout.

Step 6: Plan your lead paragraph for your newspaper article. Complete the "Newspaper Article Planner" handout.

Step 7: Write your newspaper article.

Step 8: Post your proofed and edited newspaper article on the classroom Wiki, blog, or website. (See teacher for final instructions on posting your article.)

Step 9: Complete the student section of the "Newspaper Article Project Rubric" handout.

Name: _____ Date: _____

Newspaper Article Project Rubric

Project Components	Below Proficiency 1	Nearing Proficient 2	Proficient 3	Advanced 4	Teacher Score	Student Score
Article Headline and Facts	Article is missing headline. Topic not covered; minimal supporting details.	Article has a headline that does not describe the content. Some of topic covered with minimal supporting details.	Article has a headline that accurately describes the content. Most of topic is covered with appropriate supporting details.	Article has a headline that captures the reader's attention and accurately describes the content. Topic well covered with excellent details.		
Paragraphs	Does not include topic sentence or supporting details. Very little description.	Includes topic sentence and detailed sentences. Includes few descriptions.	Includes topic sentence and detailed sentences. Includes some detailed descriptions.	Includes topic sentence and detailed sentences. Includes detailed descriptions.		
Photograph	Photograph not included in article.	Photograph included in the article, but does not depict the information in the article.	Photograph included in the article, and mostly depicts the information in the article.	Photograph included in the article, and accurately depicts the information in the article.		
Text Features	Article has few text features. Text features do not enhance the reader's understanding.	Article contains some text features that may enhance the reader's understanding.	Article contains several text features that enhance the reader's understanding.	Article contains many text features that greatly enhance the reader's understanding.		

Teacher Comments: _____

Student Comments: _____

Name: _____   Date: _____

Primary Source: Photograph Analysis

> **Title:** *The American Memory Collections*
> **Source:** Library of Congress,
> <http://www.memory.loc.gov/ammem/index.html>

Directions: Choose one photograph from the American Memory Collection at the URL above. Type "Dust Bowl" in the search box after entering the site. The photo you select will be included in your newspaper article. Use the graphic organizer below to list what you observe about the photograph.

Photograph Title: _____

Photo Citation: (Refer to the "Bibliography Guide" handout) _____

_____

People	Objects	Activities

Based on your observations, what might you infer about this image?

_____

_____

What questions does this image raise?

_____

_____

_____

Name: _____   Date: _____

Dust Bowl Research

Directions: Research the Dust Bowl era using encyclopedias, books, and the Internet.

What were some significant dates and events linked to the Dust Bowl?

Date: _____ ⟶ **Event:** _____

Date: _____ ⟶ **Event:** _____

Date: _____ ⟶ **Event:** _____

Date: _____ ⟶ **Event:** _____

What regions/states did the Dust Bowl affect? _____

_____

Describe the causes and effects of the Dust Bowl.

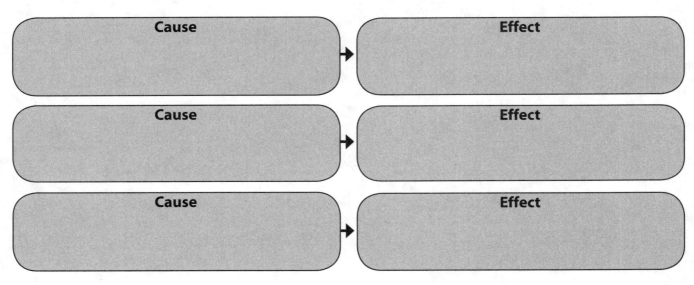

How did the Dust Bowl affect the lives of the farmers living in the Dust Bowl regions?

_____

_____

_____

Cite your sources. (Refer to Bibliography Guide)

Source: _____

_____

Source: _____

_____

Source: _____

_____

Writing a Newspaper Article

Newspaper articles reveal all the important information in the opening paragraph. It contains the *who, what, when, where, why*, and *how* of the news story.

A newspaper article includes five parts:

Headline: A short attention-getting phrase about the event.

Byline: Tells who wrote the story. For example; By Jane Smith

Lead Paragraph: Writer must find answers to *who, what, when, where, why*, and *how*.

Explanation: This section has other facts or details the reader might want to know.

Additional Background Information: This section will include several brief paragraphs explaining events leading up to the picture, related national stories, etc.

It is helpful to picture an upside-down pyramid when writing a newspaper article.

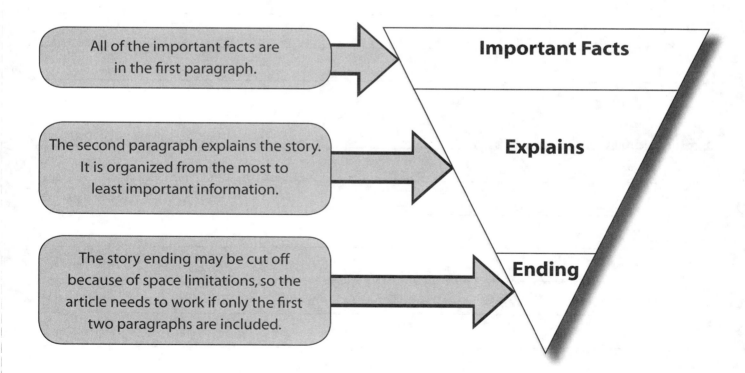

All of the important facts are in the first paragraph.

Important Facts

The second paragraph explains the story. It is organized from the most to least important information.

Explains

The story ending may be cut off because of space limitations, so the article needs to work if only the first two paragraphs are included.

Ending

Name: _____ Date: _____

Newspaper Article Planner

Directions: Use your photograph and research about the Dust Bowl era to write a newspaper article. Fill in the planner with the information you will be including in the lead paragraph of the article. Note: This is only for the first paragraph of your article; the total length of your article will depend on the other information you include.

Headline: _____

Byline: _____

Lead Paragraph

    Who: _____

    What: _____

    When: _____

    Where: _____

    Why: _____

    _____

    How: _____

    _____

Explanation: _____

_____

_____

_____

_____

_____

_____